Muslim Scientists

IBN BATTUTA
The Great Traveller

Published by Ali Gator Productions
Copyright © 2021 Ali Gator Productions, Second Edition,
First Published 2017

National Library of Australia Cataloguing–in-Publication (CIP) data:
Ahmed Imam
ISBN: 978-1-921772-38-2
For primary school age, Juvenile fiction, Dewey Number: 823.92

Adapted from the original title Ilmuan Muslim Ibnu Batutah first published by Pelangi Mizan.
Copyright © 2015 by Author Risma Dewi, Illustrator Nano. Printed in Indonesia.

T: +61 (3) 9386 2771
P.O. Box 2536, Regent West, Melbourne Victoria, 3072 Australia
E: info@ali-gator.com W: www.ali-gator.com

ALi GATOR

بِسْمِ اللهِ الرَّحْمَنِ الرَّحِيمِ

BISMILLAHIR RAHMANIR RAHIM

IN THE NAME OF ALLAH, MOST GRACIOUS, MOST MERCIFUL

Inspiring our children to learn about
the great Muslim scientists, scholars
and adventurers from
the Golden Age of Islam.

NOTES TO PARENTS AND TEACHERS

The Muslim Scientists Series aims to introduce to young readers some of the famous Muslim scientists, scholars and adventurers who discovered and invented many things that we use today and take for granted.

It is our hope that young children will be inspired by these amazing people and be encouraged to pursue their own path of discovery and questioning. It all starts with a passion for learning.

Whilst reading about Ibn Battuta, "The Great Traveller", discuss with the children about how different it must have been travelling in the time of Ibn Battuta. What do they think the differences are compared to today ?

If they were going on a long trip like Ibn Battuta, what would they take with them ? Ask them how do you think Ibn Battuta communicated with all the different people he met in different countries ? Where would they like to travel to and why ?

In Sha Allah (God Willing) if this series helps to inspire our young readers to be the next generation of thinkers, to better mankind through inventions and discoveries, then we have truly met our goal.

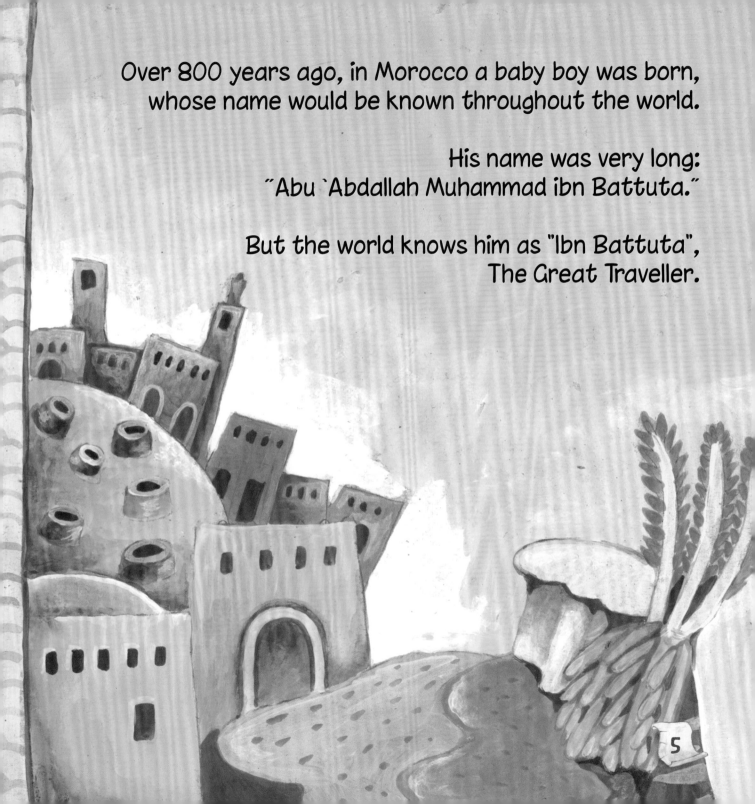

Over 800 years ago, in Morocco a baby boy was born, whose name would be known throughout the world.

His name was very long:
"Abu `Abdallah Muhammad ibn Battuta."

But the world knows him as "Ibn Battuta", The Great Traveller.

In those days, there were no cars or trains, or even planes to travel long distances.

Yet Ibn Battuta still wanted to travel to far away lands and see the world.

Ibn Battuta was inspired by the Hadith of the Prophet Muhammad (PBUH), that says:

"Whoever walks a path seeking knowledge, Allah will make easy for him the path to Paradise."*

So in the year 1325, at only 21 years of age Ibn Battuta started out on what would become a 30 year journey.

* Sahih Muslim

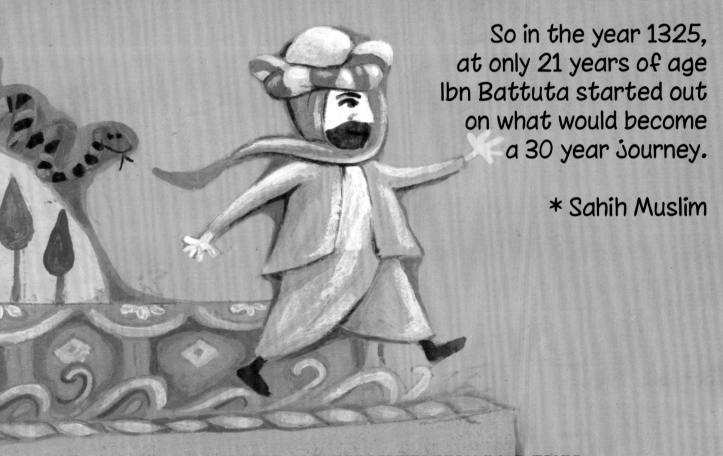

HADITH - SAYING OF THE PROPHET MUHAMMAD (PBUH)

PBUH - PEACE BE UPON HIM

Ibn Battuta wanted his journey
to be full of Barakah.

So his first goal was to go to
the Holy City of Makkah
to perform Hajj.

He started out alone,
but soon found other Muslims
going to perform the Hajj.

So he joined them for this
long trip across the
desert to Makkah.

BARAKAH – BLESSINGS FROM ALLAH
HAJJ - PILGRIMAGE

11

As Ibn Battuta travelled across the globe he met many different people, from different cultures and religions.

He always respected their culture as he was a guest in their city and he stayed strong with his Islam.

Ibn Battuta actually performed Hajj four times during his long journey.

Ibn Battuta's travels
took him up and down and
across the world.

Through Africa, Eastern Europe,
The Middle East, India, Central Asia,
Southeast Asia and China.

14

His incredible journey covered
over 73,000 miles / 117,000 kilometers.

Ibn Battuta even went all the way down to what is today Indonesia, to the city of Aceh.

That's a long way from Morocco!

After travelling for an amazing 30 years
Ibn Battuta finally arrived back home
to Tangiers, Morocco.

Here he began recording his fabulous adventure in
a journal called AL RIHLA "The Journey".

Today it can be seen in
the French National Library in Paris.

Ibn Battuta's journey took him all over the world. He could only achieve this with the blessing of Allah.

Ibn Battuta was always grateful that Allah protected him throughout his journey.

Be your trip long or short, your safety and success is fully controlled by Allah.

Get a map of the world and look to see where you would like to visit.

Would you like to go to Makkah like Ibn Battuta ?

What do you think it was like travelling by horse or camel across these lands like Ibn Battuta did ?

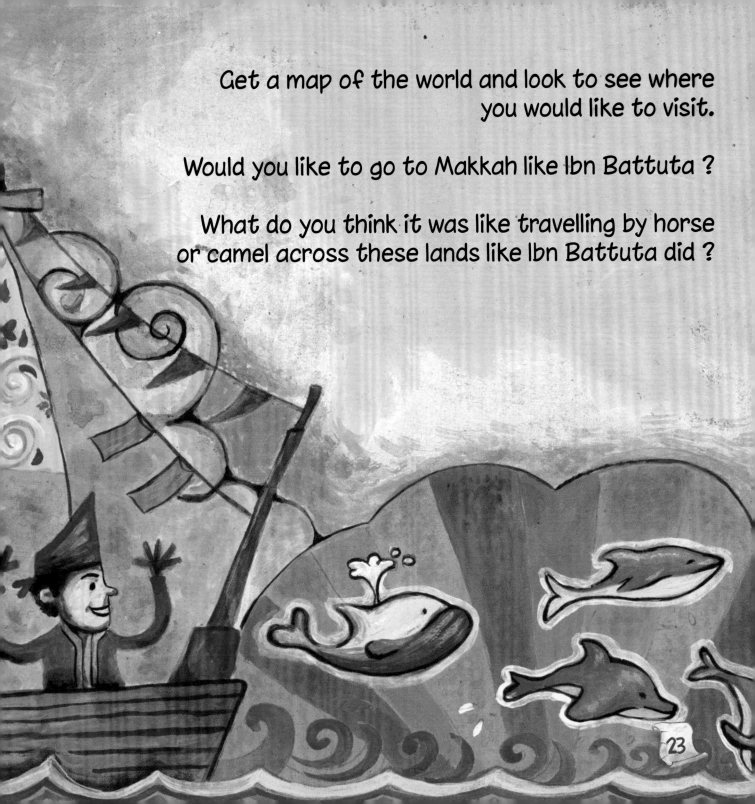

الحَمْدُ لِلَّهِ

ALHAMDULILLAH - PRAISE BE TO ALLAH

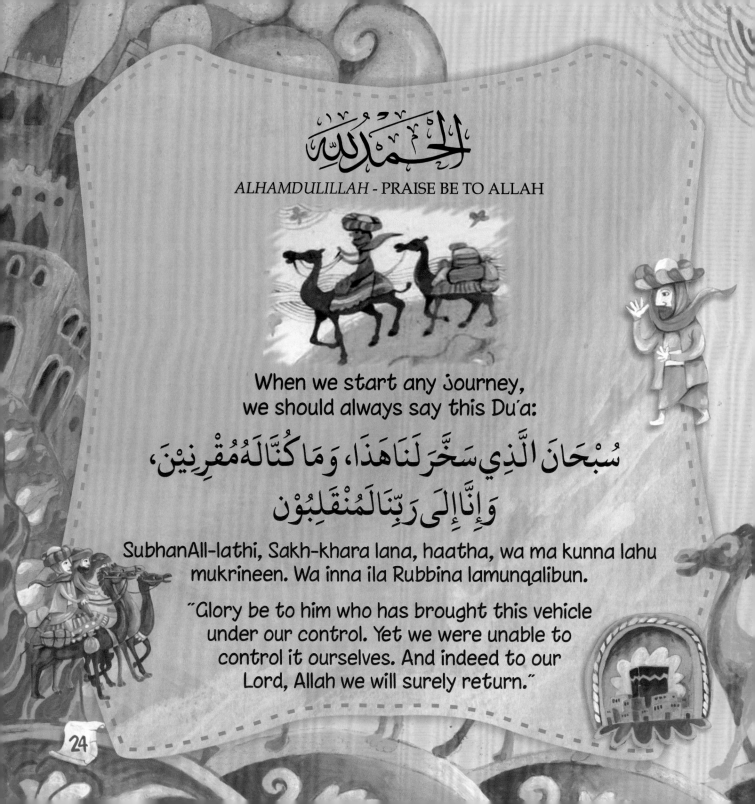

When we start any journey,
we should always say this Du'a:

سُبْحَانَ الَّذِي سَخَّرَ لَنَا هَذَا، وَمَا كُنَّا لَهُ مُقْرِنِينَ،
وَإِنَّا إِلَى رَبِّنَا لَمُنْقَلِبُوْن

SubhanAll-lathi, Sakh-khara lana, haatha, wa ma kunna lahu
mukrineen. Wa inna ila Rubbina lamunqalibun.

"Glory be to him who has brought this vehicle
under our control. Yet we were unable to
control it ourselves. And indeed to our
Lord, Allah we will surely return."